My First Book of
PSALMS

Susan Jones

Good Books
New York, New York

Good Books books may be purchased in bulk at special discounts for sales promotion, corporate gifts, fund-raising, or educational purposes. Special editions can also be created to specifications. For details, contact the Special Sales Department, Good Books, 307 West 36th Street, 11th Floor, New York, NY 10018 or info@skyhorsepublishing.com.

Good Books is an imprint of Skyhorse Publishing, Inc.®, a Delaware corporation.

Visit our website at www.goodbooks.com.

10 9 8 7 6 5 4 3 2 1

Library of Congress Cataloging-in-Publication Data is available on file.

Cover and interior art used under license from Shutterstock.com.

Print ISBN: 978-1-68099-321-9
Ebook ISBN: 978-1-68099-327-1

Printed in China

How to Use This Book

It's never too early to learn about the Bible and its teachings. *My First Book of Psalms* is a fun way to introduce your little one to the beauty of these timeless songs of praise. Inside you'll find 30 inspiring Bible verses along with modern, kid-friendly explanations to help clarify each verse's meaning for children of all ages.

Begin by having your child listen as you read a few lines of a cherished Psalm out loud. Encourage your little one to repeat the words along with you. Make learning fun: Be generous with your praise and give children plenty of chances to get the words just right. When a child succeeds in learning a verse by heart, he or she may choose a special sticker as a reward! Help them find the matching sticker on the enclosed sticker pages and cheer their efforts as they place it in the space provided. Depending on your child's age, consider introducing a new verse every week—soon they will be able to recite dozens of Bible verses by heart.

Don't forget to celebrate every one of your child's successes with a big hug and loving words of encouragement. Enjoy sharing elements of your faith each and every day and adding the comfort of God's love and guidance to your child's expanding world.

Our help is in the name of the Lord,
who made heaven and earth.

—PSALM 124:8

God is always on your side. We know that God is powerful because he made everything here on earth and everything up in heaven. Whenever you are sad or need help, just remember that God is with you making you stronger.

Sing to him a new song;
play skillfully,
and shout for joy.

—PSALM 33:3

Your joy and praise is a beautiful gift to God. Celebrate God and show everyone around you how happy you are to have Him in your life. It feels good to sing, pray, or talk to someone about your love for God!

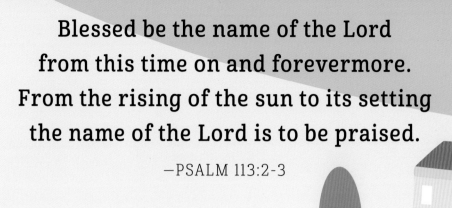

Blessed be the name of the Lord
from this time on and forevermore.
From the rising of the sun to its setting
the name of the Lord is to be praised.

—PSALM 113:2-3

You celebrate God's glory every time you say his name with love. His presence in our lives is a true blessing.

Praise the Lord!
Praise God in his sanctuary;
praise him in his mighty heavens!
Praise him for his mighty deeds;
praise him according to
his excellent greatness!

—PSALM 150

There are many ways to praise God. You can do it in church, at home—even on the playground! He is amazing in so many ways and He will always listen when you talk to Him.

Give thanks to the Lord, for he is good,
for his steadfast love endures forever.
Give thanks to the God of gods,
for his steadfast love endures forever.
Give thanks to the Lord of lords,
for his steadfast love endures forever.

—PSALM 136:1-3

One of the best things about God's love is that it has no end. It's there for you when you need it as you change and grow.

Make a joyful noise to the Lord, all the earth.
Worship the Lord with gladness;
come into his presence with singing.

—PSALMS 100:1-2

When your heart is filled with love for God,
you want to sing it out for everyone to hear.
Everywhere on Earth people are singing God's praises.

It is good to give thanks to the Lord,
to sing praises to your name, O Most High;
to declare your steadfast love in the morning,
and your faithfulness by night.

—PSALM 92:1-2

Any time of day is a good time of day to think of God. When you're brushing your teeth in the morning or when you're settling into bed at night, send a message of thanks to God.

He who dwells in the shelter of the Most High will abide in the shadow of the Almighty. I will say to the Lord, "My refuge and my fortress, my God, in whom I trust."

—PSALM 91:1-2

The Lord will protect you when you need it.
Having faith in God is like having
an umbrella to shield you from the rain.

I will sing of the steadfast love of the Lord, forever; with my mouth I will make known your faithfulness to all generations.

—PSALM 89:1

You can trust God. He loves us always and keeps His promises to never leave our sides. When you feel like others are letting you down, you can always turn to God.

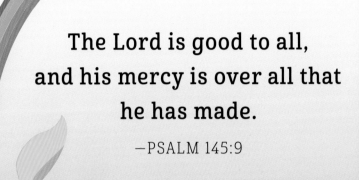

The Lord is good to all,
and his mercy is over all that
he has made.

—PSALM 145:9

God doesn't play favorites.
We're all on His team, if we want
to be. All you need to do is love
and follow Him.

Give thanks to the Lord, for he is good, for his steadfast love endures forever.

—PSALM 136:1

Have you ever had an amazing day that you wish would never end? That's how it is with God's love. We can never use it up like sidewalk chalk or bubbles. It stays with us forever. Be sure to let Him know how thankful you are!

When I am afraid,
I put my trust in you.
In God, whose word I praise,
in God I trust;
I shall not be afraid.

—PSALM 56:3-4

We all have fears—maybe spiders or being alone in the dark scares us. But the good news is we also all have God, who loves us and watches over us. Pray about what frightens you—God is always listening.

Behold, how good and pleasant it is
when brothers dwell in unity!

—PSALM 133:1

In the Bible, "brothers" means
the people in your community.
We make God happy when we get
along with other people like brothers,
sisters, moms and dads, grandparents,
teachers, and playmates.

In peace I will both lie down and sleep;
for you alone, O Lord,
make me dwell in safety.

—PSALM 4:8

God wants you to feel safe and full of peace,
so end the day by talking to Him. Get all of your
wiggles out during the daytime and then find
comfort at night in saying your bedtime prayers.

Declare his glory among the nations, his marvelous works among all the peoples!

—PSALM 96:3

Ever find a new movie, game, or toy you love?
You want to tell everyone about it.
When we love God so much, we should want
to share Him with others too.

Great is our Lord, and abundant in power; his understanding is beyond measure.

—PSALM 147:5

God is so powerful that He created the world and everything in it. But He's not too "big" to understand every one of our cares and needs. You can bring any problem to Him just by talking to Him in prayer!

Oh come, let us worship and bow down;
let us kneel before the Lord, our Maker!
For he is our God,
and we are the people of his pasture,
and the sheep of his hand.

—PSALM 95:6-7

God cares for us like a shepherd cares for his sheep—all day and night. Shepherds want their sheep to follow them so they can keep the sheep safe. God wants to do the same for us.

I praise you, for I am fearfully
and wonderfully made.

—PSALM 139:14

Isn't it amazing how God created us all to be one-of-a-kind? We are all God's children, but we are all unique with different gifts and talents. Thank God for how special He made you, and try to see the special gifts God gave to each person.

Blessed is the one whose transgression is forgiven.

—PSALM 32:5

Transgression is a big word that means
"mistakes" or "sins." God knows we will mess up.
The important part is not to try to hide it. We
simply say we're sorry and ask God to forgive us
and help us not to do the same thing again.

Praise the Lord, all you nations!
Exalt him, all you peoples!
For great is his gracious love toward us,
and the Lord's faithfulness is eternal.

—PSALM 117:1-2

Think of some things that you can thank God for today. Remember to look for the good in your life and not complain too much about the things you don't have. God's gracious love is the best gift in your life.

How blessed is the person,
who does not take the advice of the wicked,
who does not stand on the path with sinners,
and who does not sit in the seat of mockers.

—PSALM 1:1

The Bible teaches you what's good and right. Try your best to do what God would want you to do. Don't listen to anyone who tells you to do what you know is wrong in the eyes of God.

The Lord is my shepherd; I shall not want
He maketh me to lie down in green pastures:
he leadeth me beside the still waters.
He restoreth my soul: he leadeth me in the paths
of righteousness for his name's sake.

—PSALM 23:1-3

Know that God will take care of you. You may not get everything you want—everyone has things they want but can't have—but you will get everything you need from God. Love, protection, and guidance are some of the things we need that God gives us.

The heavens declare the glory of God, and the sky above proclaims his handiwork.

—PSALM 19

We can get a better sense of how incredible God is by looking all around us at the beauty of his creations. Stop to notice the great big sky, the mountains, the lakes, and the oceans. They are reminders of our amazing God.

Lord, our Lord,
how excellent is your name in all the earth!
You set your glory above the heavens!

—PSALM 8:1

Praising God is fun and lifts our spirits. Sometimes just saying his name can remind us of the great power of God up above.

Indeed, God is king over all the earth;
sing a song of praise.
God is king over the nations;
God is seated on his holy throne.

—PSALM 47:7-8

There is no person more powerful than God. He is more important than any ruler, because he is the creator of Heaven and Earth.

Have mercy, God,
according to your gracious love,
according to your unlimited compassion,
erase my transgressions.
Wash me from my iniquity,
cleanse me from my sin.

—PSALM 51:1-1

You can ask God to "erase" your mistakes by asking for forgiveness. He knows that you are young and still learning about right and wrong. God's gracious love always gives you another chance to make things right.

Sing aloud to God our strength;
shout for joy to the God of Jacob.
Raise a song, sound the tambourine,
the sweet lyre with the harp.

—PSALM 81:1-2

When we feel tired or confused or sad, our faith in God helps us feel stronger. Singing a song and playing an instrument is one way to get God's attention to thank Him for making you feel stronger. Plus, it's fun!

More majestic than the thunders of mighty waters,more majestic than the waves of the sea, majestic on high is the Lord!

—PSALM 81:1-2

There's nothing on Earth mightier than the Lord. Nothing can match his power and glory—not even the huge waves in the ocean.

How can young people keep their way pure?
By guarding it according to your word.
With my whole heart I seek you;
do not let me stray from your commandments.

—PSALM 119:9-10

Commandments are God's most important rules to follow. Seeking God with your heart means reading the Bible with your parents and trying to live by God's rules.

Happy is everyone who fears the Lord,
who walks in his ways.
You shall eat the fruit of the labor of your hands;
you shall be happy, and it shall go well with you.
Your wife will be like a fruitful vine
within your house; your children will be like
olive shoots around your table.

—PSALM 128:1-3

Believing in the strength and power of God holds families together and makes them happy. When one member of your family "walks in God's way" by following God's teaching, it inspires everyone else to do the same.